Texas Driver License Exam

"You never fail until you stop trying" - Albert Einstein

For inquiries;
info@xmprep.com

Texas Driver License Exam #1

Test Taking Tips

☐ Take a deep breath and relax

☐ Read directions carefully

☐ Read the questions thoroughly

☐ Make sure you understand what is being asked

☐ Go over all of the choices before you answer

☐ Paraphrase the question

☐ Eliminate the options you know are wrong

☐ Check your work

☐ Think positively and do your best

Table of Contents

TEST DIRECTION

DIRECTIONS

Read the questions carefully and then choose the ONE best answer to each question.

Be sure to allocate your time carefully so you are able to complete the entire test within the testing session. You may go back and review your answers at any time.

You may use any available space in your test booklet for scratch work.

Questions in this booklet are not actual test questions but they are the samples for commonly asked questions.

This test aims to cover all topics which may appear on the actual test. However some topics may not be covered.

Studying this booklet will be preparing you for the actual test. It will not guarantee improving your test score but it will help you pass your exam on the first attempt.

Some useful tips for answering multiple choice questions;

- Start with the questions that you can easily answer.

- Underline the keywords in the question.

- Be sure to read all the choices given.

- Watch for keywords such as NOT, always, only, all, never, completely.

- Do not forget to answer every question.

CONTINUE ▶

1

What happens if a driver is slowing down just to look at collisions or anything else out of the ordinary?

A) The driver is causing traffic congestion.

B) The driver is improving the traffic flow by preventing collisions.

C) The driver is preventing rear-end collisions.

D) The driver is practicing safety precaution.

2

An old man with a guide dog is at the corner ready to cross the street in front of you. Yet, you want to make a right turn at the corner.

What should you do before making your right turn?

A) You should wait until the old man crosses the street.

B) Tell the old man when to cross the street.

C) Turn your engine off until the old man crosses the street.

D) Keep sounding your horn so that the old man is warned.

3

What should you do if you see orange construction signs and cones on a freeway?

A) You should slow down because the lane ends ahead.

B) You should maintain your current speed and change lanes.

C) You should be prepared for construction workers and equipment ahead.

D) You should increase your speed because you are on a danger zone.

4

In the above image, what does the double solid yellow line mean?

A) Traffic is moving in the same direction.

B) Passing is allowed.

C) Passing is NOT allowed.

D) Traffic is moving in high speed.

5

What does the traffic sign illustrated above means?

A) No U-turn
B) No left turn
C) No stopping
D) Detour ahead

6

Which of the following would be a safe choice if you have taken too many drinks?

A) Waiting an hour for each drink
B) Taking a cold shower
C) Drinking coffee
D) Asking someone who has not been drinking to drive

CONTINUE ▶

7

As you were driving along a street, you heard a siren, but you could not immediately see the emergency vehicle.

Which of the following would be the most appropriate action in this situation?

A) You should pull to the curb and check if it is on your street.

B) You should continue driving until you see the emergency vehicle.

C) You should speed up and turn at the next intersection.

D) You should slow down but don't stop until you see it.

8

In most States, a speed limit ban is issued towards the urban district area where there is a lack of cars. Drivers tend to speed up when the streets are less crowded.

Which of the following refers to the speed limit issued for Texas drivers in urban districts?

A) 30 mph

B) 35 mph

C) 40 mph

D) 60 mph

9

For a Driving While Intoxicated (DWI) case, the driver will be suspended and fined according to the number of offense made. The license will be confiscated and will be released after the suspension period.

Which of the following is the amount that is stated to be paid for the third offense for a driver convicted of DWI?

A) $2,000.00

B) $4,000.00

C) $8,000.00

D) $10,000.00

10

Which of the following is true about checking your rearview mirrors while driving?

A) Check your rearview mirror so that you can see if a car is in your blind spot.

B) Check your rearview mirror only when you are slowing down.

C) Check your rearview mirror to see how traffic is moving behind.

D) Check your rearview mirror only when you are in high speed.

11

Which of the following is the best thing to do if you are waiting in the intersection to complete a left turn?

A) You should give a signal and keep your wheels turned to the left.

B) You should flash your headlights so that the driver will let you get through.

C) You should give a signal and keep your wheels straight.

D) You should drive around the rear of a car if it blocks you.

12

What does the bicyclist want to tell you on his signal as shown above?

A) Stopping

B) Turning left

C) Turning right

D) Speeding

13

What happens if you are driving faster than the other cars on the road with one lane in each direction and continuously passing the other cars?

A) You are helping to prevent traffic congestion.

B) You will arrive to your destination much faster and safer.

C) You are increasing your chances of an accident.

D) You are decreasing the probability of an accident.

14

Which of the following circumstances is true?

A) You have the right-of-way when you are already in a traffic circle.

B) You have the right-of-way when you are entering a traffic circle.

C) You have the right-of-way when you are leaving a parking space.

D) You have the right-of-way when you are backing out of a driveway.

15

What should you do if you see that a dust storm is coming in your way or you encounter one while driving?

A) You should decrease your speed, carefully pull off the road, switch off the lights, remove your foot on the brake and wait until the dust storm passes.

B) You should decrease your speed, carefully pull off the road, switch on the lights and wait until the dust storm passes.

C) You should be cautious and drive through the dust storm since it usually doesn't last very long.

D) You should drive faster to avoid the dust storm.

16

A driver under the age of 21 is under the influence of alcohol. The law enforcement cited the driver for a DUI (Driving Under Intoxication) and required to perform up to 40 hours of community service.

Which of the following is the fine in Texas for the offense cited above?

A) $100.00

B) $300.00

C) $500.00

D) $1,000.00

CONTINUE ▶

17

When can you say if it is safe to pass another vehicle?

A) When you are entering a curve and there are no approaching vehicles.

B) When you are traveling through an intersection and there are no oncoming vehicles.

C) Whenever there are signs and/or roadway markings that permit passing other vehicles.

D) When there is a sharp curve on the road

18

What is the first thing that a drink of alcohol affects?

A) Vision

B) Judgment and skills

C) Balance

D) Immune system

19

Where do you think you are driving if you are traveling in the far right lane of a four-lane freeway and you observe thick broken white lines on the left side of your lane?

A) You are driving in an exit lane.

B) You are traveling in a special lane for slow moving vehicles.

C) You are driving in the carpool lane and must merge into the next lane.

D) You are traveling in a special lane for fast moving trucks.

20

Which of the following situations is correct?

A) You may overtake another vehicle on the right if it is waiting to turn left.

B) You may overtake another vehicle on the right if it is waiting to park at the curb.

C) You may overtake another vehicle on the right if it is waiting to turn right.

D) You may overtake another vehicle on the right if it is waiting to turn into a driveway on the right.

21

What will happen as the percentage of alcohol (BAC) in your blood increases?

A) You become more coordinated as BAC increases.

B) You become more sober as BAC increases.

C) You become more intoxicated as BAC increases.

D) You become more focused as BAC increases.

22

Which of the following is affected by alcohol?

A) Reaction time

B) Judgment of distances

C) Recovery from headlight glare

D) All of the above

23

Which of the following should be obeyed first by a driver?

A) A flashing red light

B) A stop sign

C) A policeman

D) A steady red light

24

When are you allowed to cross a double, yellow line when overtaking another car?

A) When the yellow line next to the other side of the road is a broken line

B) When the yellow line next to your side of the road is a broken line

C) When the yellow line next to the other side of the road is a solid line

D) When the yellow line next to your side of the road is a solid line

25

A blood alcohol content (BAC) of 0.08% or higher is considered legally impaired.

Which of the following methods can effectively reduce your BAC?

A) Giving your body time to get rid of alcohol

B) Taking a cold shower

C) Exercising moderately

D) Drinking coffee

26

Children below the height of 4'9" in Texas are required to be seated in a dedicated child passenger safety seat. If caught for violating, a fine not more than $250.00 can be charged.

Which of the following age will the law be also applicable?

A) Below 8 years old

B) Below 9 years old

C) Below 10 years old

D) Below 12 years old

27

Which of the following must a bicyclist on a roadway should do?

A) The bicyclist must ride on either side of the road.

B) The bicyclist must ride on the side of the road facing traffic.

C) The bicyclist must ride on the right side of the road.

D) The bicyclist must ride on the side of the road with the least traffic.

28

Which of the following will happen if you drink coffee after drinking alcohol?

A) It cancels the effect of the alcohol.

B) It decreases blood alcohol content.

C) It has no effect on blood alcohol content.

D) It increases blood alcohol content.

CONTINUE ▶

29

What should a driver who is taking a non-prescription drug do?

A) Check and read the labels on the drug before driving.

B) He should just continue to drive.

C) He should drive only during daylight hours.

D) He should drink alcohol instead.

30

Rainfall is one of the reasons why roadways become slippery.

In which of the following circumstances are roadways the most slippery?

A) The first rain after a dry spell

B) After raining for a while

C) When it is raining cats and dogs

D) When the wet road has dried

31

What does the road sign given above mean?

A) No entrance

B) No right turn

C) No U-Turn

D) No left turn

32

What is the meaning of the road sign illustrated above?

A) Yield right-of-way

B) Reduction in lanes

C) No passing zone

D) Intersection ahead

33

Which of the following should bicyclists do when traveling on the highway?

A) Bicyclists should ride facing traffic.
B) Bicyclists should abide the same laws as drivers.
C) Bicyclists must stay in the right lane.
D) Bicyclist must stay in the left lane.

34

When is a driver allowed to drive near or under a gate that is being lowered or raised at a railroad crossing?

A) If the driver carefully looks first in both directions.
B) Under no circumstances.
C) As long as the incoming train is not too close.
D) If the driver's vehicle can do so without damaging the gate.

35

You want to back out of your driveway, however, you see kids playing nearby.

Which of the following should you do before you start moving your car?

A) You should race your motor to warn the children that you are moving.
B) You should walk to the back of the car to be sure the way is clear.
C) You should tell the children to stay away from the driveway.
D) You should sound your horn so the children will hear you.

36

What should you do if you come to an intersection which has a flashing red light?

A) You should only stop if cars are already in the intersection.
B) You should only stop if cars are approaching the intersection.
C) You should decrease your speed and be prepared to stop if necessary.
D) You should first come to a full stop, then go when safe to do so.

37

Which of the following is the most appropriate action if a driver wants to turn left at an intersection where light is green and the oncoming traffic is heavy?

A) The driver may take the right-of-way since he has the light.

B) The driver may use the next intersection.

C) The driver should wait at the crosswalk for the traffic to clear.

D) The driver should wait at the center of the intersection until the traffic is clear.

38

Which of the following factors affects the absorption of alcohol of an individual?

A) Weight

B) Height

C) Race

D) Gender

39

Which of the following is the meaning of the traffic sign shown above?

A) The way curves ahead.

B) Merging traffic from the right ahead.

C) There is an intersection ahead.

D) Traffic is one-way ahead.

40

What is the most appropriate thing to do before leaving a parking space which is parallel to the curb?

A) The driver should look for traffic by turning his head.

B) The driver should turn on the four-way flasher.

C) The driver should look for traffic by using the inside rear-view mirror.

D) The driver should sound the horn.

CONTINUE ▶

SECTION 1

#	Answer	Topic	Subtopic	#	Answer	Topic	Subtopic	#	Answer	Topic	Subtopic	#	Answer	Topic	Subtopic
1	A	T03	S03676	11	C	T03	S03674	21	C	T03	S03673	31	D	T03	S03674
2	A	T03	S03675	12	A	T03	S03674	22	D	T03	S03673	32	A	T03	S03674
3	C	T03	S03674	13	C	T03	S03676	23	C	T03	S03675	33	B	T03	S03675
4	C	T03	S03674	14	A	T03	S03675	24	B	T03	S03675	34	B	T03	S03676
5	A	T03	S03674	15	A	T03	S03676	25	A	T03	S03673	35	B	T03	S03676
6	D	T03	S03673	16	C	T44	S44837	26	A	T44	S44839	36	D	T03	S03674
7	A	T03	S03676	17	C	T03	S03675	27	C	T03	S03676	37	D	T03	S03674
8	A	T44	S44839	18	B	T03	S03673	28	C	T03	S03673	38	A	T03	S03673
9	D	T44	S44837	19	A	T03	S03675	29	A	T03	S03673	39	B	T03	S03674
10	C	T03	S03676	20	A	T03	S03676	30	A	T03	S03676	40	A	T03	S03676

Topics & Subtopics

Code	Description	Code	Description
S03	USA DMV	S03676	Safety
S03673	Alcohol and Drug	S44	TX DMV
S03674	Road Signs	S44837	Alcohol and Drug
S03675	Rules and Laws	S44839	Rules and Laws

CONTINUE ▶

TEST DIRECTION

DIRECTIONS

Read the questions carefully and then choose the ONE best answer to each question.

Be sure to allocate your time carefully so you are able to complete the entire test within the testing session. You may go back and review your answers at any time.

You may use any available space in your test booklet for scratch work.

Questions in this booklet are not actual test questions but they are the samples for commonly asked questions.

This test aims to cover all topics which may appear on the actual test. However some topics may not be covered.

Studying this booklet will be preparing you for the actual test. It will not guarantee improving your test score but it will help you pass your exam on the first attempt.

Some useful tips for answering multiple choice questions;

- Start with the questions that you can easily answer.

- Underline the keywords in the question.

- Be sure to read all the choices given.

- Watch for keywords such as NOT, always, only, all, never, completely.

- Do not forget to answer every question.

1

What does the sign given above mean?

A) Beginning of a divided highway

B) End of an interstate highway

C) Slippery road ahead

D) Intersection ahead

2

Vehicles on the road may carry a sign to indicate its purpose. Some vehicles are required to put insignia or other symbols to help other people determine what type of vehicle it is while on the road.

Which of the following refers to the sign on the image given above?

A) Vehicle that is carrying toxic materials

B) Law enforcement vehicle

C) Passenger vehicle

D) Slow moving vehicle

3

Driving While Intoxicated, or simply DWI, is a serious driving offense which includes suspension of driving license and a large amount of fine in Texas.

Which of the following should be the longest length of time a driver can be sentenced to jail for the first offense?

A) 360 days

B) 180 days

C) 90 days

D) 60 days

4

As you are driving, you notice that there is no crosswalk and you see a man crossing your lane ahead. Which of the following should you do?

A) Slow down as you pass him.

B) Stop and wait until he finishes crossing the street.

C) Make eye contact and then pass him.

D) Sound your horn aggresively to notify him.

CONTINUE ▶

5

It is a common occurrence that police officers often stop cars in Texas. It is done for inspections and checks or other causes.

Which of the following refers to the action that a driver should do when stopped by a police officer?

A) Turn on the hazard lights
B) Turn off the car engine
C) Pull over to the right side
D) All of the above

6

Which of the following is a correct action if you are approaching a green traffic light but traffic is blocking the intersection?

A) Do not enter the junction until you can get completely across.
B) You may partially enter the junction to establish your right-of-way.
C) You may continue into the intersection and wait for traffic to clear.
D) You may continue driving into the intersection to block vehicles still attempting to cross the intersection.

7

When you witnessed a collision scene, which of the following is the best thing to do?

A) You should help move the injured, even if they're not in a burning vehicle or in immediate danger.
B) You should try to remove power lines, if there are power lines down with wires in the road.
C) You should stand or walk in traffic lanes to wait for help to arrive.
D) You should stop your vehicle near the collision site. If you can move your vehicle, get it off the road.

8

Which of the following is correct about a right turn on red?

A) It is only allowed on a divided road.
B) It is permitted on any roads except when there is a sign that it is prohibited.
C) It is only allowed on roads where there is a sign that right turn is permitted.
D) It is only allowed on roads where there is a sign that left turn is permitted.

9

While driving, you observed a solid yellow line next to a broken yellow line on the road. What is the meaning of those lines?

A) It means that you may pass on both directions.

B) It means that you may pass next to the solid line.

C) It means that you may pass next to the broken line.

D) It means that you should keep driving on your lane.

10

What is the purpose of having extra space when driving in front of a large truck?

A) It is needed for the truck driver to stop the vehicle.

B) It is needed for the other drivers when they want to slow down.

C) It is needed for the other drivers when merging onto a freeway.

D) It is needed for the other drivers when they want to speed up.

11

What is the meaning of the road sign shown above?

A) Divided highway ahead

B) Intersection ahead

C) Four-lane traffic ahead

D) Two-way traffic ahead

12

A car was stopped in Texas, and the officer saw that a 16-year-old passenger was in the car while not wearing his seat belt.

Which of the following should be fined and cited under Chapter 14 of the Texas Driver Handbook?

A) The driver only

B) The passenger only

C) The passenger and the driver

D) Neither the passenger nor the driver

CONTINUE ▶

During good weather conditions, drivers are subjected to the two-second rule. The distance must be maintained to ensure safety in case there are unexpected accidents or emergencies in the vehicle ahead.

Which of the following should be the count followed when driving in a bad weather condition?

A) 3 seconds

B) 5 seconds

C) 8 seconds

D) 10 seconds

Aggressive driver is an act of a motorist in a hostile and unsafe manner without considering the other motorists on the road.

How can someone identify aggressive drivers?

A) Through their tendency to drive slow

B) When a driver keeps on shifting lanes erratically and improperly

C) Through the number of passengers in their car

D) Through their tendency to drive at the same speed with the traffic

CONTINUE ▶

15

Implied consent laws say that by just driving on the road, you are agreeing to take a chemical test to assess your BAC.

If you unlawfully refuse to take a chemical test either through breath or blood test, what will happen?

A) Your driver's license will be taken away.

B) There is no proof to find you guilty of drunk driving.

C) You cannot be arrested for drunk driving.

D) You will probably face serious consequences worse than if you were just found guilty of driving under the influence.

16

What is the meaning of the sign given above?

A) Warning

B) Signal ahead

C) Railroad crossing

D) Stop

17

Which of the following should you inspect to see vehicles in your blind spot?

A) The inside rearview mirror

B) The outside rearview mirror

C) Over your shoulders

D) Look at the back

18

Which of the following is the meaning of the road sign shown above?

A) Yield right-of-way

B) Stop

C) Traffic signal ahead

D) Crossroad ahead

19

Which of the following is the most appropriate thing to do when you want to overtake and pass another vehicle?

A) You should give a signal and pass when safe to do so.

B) You should wait for a signal from the other driver.

C) You should change lanes quickly so the other driver will see you.

D) You should stay close behind so you need less time to pass.

20

What does the sign given above mean?

A) Hiking trails ahead to the right

B) Hotel ahead to the right

C) Highway changes ahead to the right

D) Hospital ahead to the right

21

Road rage is an aggressive behavior exhibited by a driver which includes rude gestures, verbal insults.

What can you do to reduce "road rage"?

A) Use your horn frequently.

B) Talk on your cell phone while driving.

C) Turn on the radio.

D) Always signal your intention when changing lanes.

22

Being a driver, which of the following statements is correct?

A) The distance you need to cross traffic depends on the presence of a stop sign.

B) The distance you need to cross traffic depends on the use of your turn signals.

C) The distance you need to cross traffic depends on the road, oncoming traffic and weather conditions.

D) The distance you need to cross traffic depends on the cars behind you.

CONTINUE ▶

23

While driving on the freeway, you are in the same lane with a large truck and you are behind it. Which of the following should you do in this case?

A) You should drive with a greater distance behind the truck than for a passenger vehicle.

B) You should drive closer behind the large truck than for a passenger vehicle.

C) You should drive at the right side of the truck and wait for it to pass,

D) You should drive at the left side of the truck and overtake.

24

Which of the following is true about driving and drinking alcohol?

A) Driving and drinking alcohol is a serious traffic safety problem.

B) Driving and drinking alcohol is only dangerous to the driver who drinks.

C) Driving and drinking alcohol is a minor traffic safety problem.

D) Driving and drinking alcohol is safe if you only have a few drinks.

25

What does the bicyclist want to tell you by his signal as shown above?

A) Debris in roadway

B) Stopping

C) Turning left

D) Turning right

26

What is the best thing that you should do if you encounter a mechanical problem with your vehicle?

A) You should stop in your lane and turn on your hazard lights.

B) You should pull off the road and switch on your hazard lights.

C) You should give a signal and pull into the slow lane.

D) You should stop in your lane and wait until the towing truck arrives.

CONTINUE ▶

27

A driver's crash report (DCR) in Texas is a filed report (within ten days from the date of the incident) by the driver for an accident/crash that was not investigated under law enforcement resulting into injury, death, or damage to properties.

Which of the following is the minimum amount of damage to properties that should be involved before filing a DCR?

A) $100.00

B) $500.00

C) $1,000.00

D) $2,000.00

28

What does the road sign shown above mean?

A) Soft shoulders for motorcycles

B) Yield right-of-way

C) Stop only if other cars are approaching.

D) Bicycles can cross or ride beside traffic.

29

Which of the following is the effect of alcohol and another drug combined in your blood?

A) It can reduce the effects of alcohol.

B) It can reduce the effects of the drug or medicine.

C) Both have no effect on driving ability.

D) It increases the effects of alcohol and drug.

30

What does it mean if you see the sign shown above along your lane?

A) You may not exit the freeway.

B) You may keep driving in this lane and continue through the interchange.

C) You may exit the freeway in this lane or continue through the interchange.

D) If you stay in this lane, you must exit the freeway.

31

What is the typical school zone speed limit when approaching a school crossing?

A) 5 mph
B) 15 mph
C) 45 mph
D) 55 mph

32

Which of the following is the proper way of making a right turn?

A) The driver must slow down and get into the lane nearest the centerline.

B) The driver must give a signal and get into the lane nearest the left curb.

C) The driver should approach the corner of the lane nearest to the right curb, but drive towards the middle of the street before turning.

D) The driver must give a signal and get into the lane nearest the right curb.

33

Drivers that enter a road construction area must follow the road signs promptly. It is recommended to slow down and take the time to check the road signs to maintain the safety of both the driver and the workers.

Which of the following is indicated on the road sign in the picture given above?

A) Construction is underway
B) People are present ahead
C) Workers near the roadway
D) Street cleaners are cleaning ahead

34

While driving, you saw that a school bus is stopped, and its red lights are flashing. What does this mean?

A) You may pass if there are no children on the road.

B) You are not allowed to pass if the bus is on the other side of a divided highway.

C) You may pass if the the front of the bus is what you are facing.

D) You are not allowed to pass while the red lights are flashing.

35

If you noticed a white line on the right edge of the highway slanting towards your left, what does it tell you?

A) You are required to turn left just ahead.

B) There is an intersection just ahead.

C) You are approaching a construction area.

D) The road will get narrower.

36

Consider the situation wherein a pedestratian starts to cross the street after the "Don't walk" signal appears. Then, your signal light changes to green while the pedestrian is still in the middle of the street.

Which of the following should you do?

A) You may get going if the pedestrian is not in your lane anymore.

B) You should wait and see until the pedestrian crosses the street before you start driving.

C) You may proceed if you have the right of way.

D) You should sound your horn continuously.

37

Which of the following should you do if an oncoming vehicle has its high beams switched on making it difficult to see the road ahead?

A) Take a look ahead toward the right edge of your lane.

B) Take a look ahead toward the left edge of your lane.

C) Take a look straight ahead in your lane.

D) Take a look at the back of your car to avoid the light.

38

Defensive driving is a set of road skills, and strategies that assist the driver in defending himself against possible collisions.

Which of the following is one of the rules of defensive driving?

A) Stay alert and keep your eyes moving.

B) Look straight ahead as you drive.

C) Anticipate that other drivers will make up for your errors.

D) Believe that you can avoid danger at the last minute.

39

Road signs in the USA also include signs for animals. There are cases like this as well in other countries for their sheep or cattle.

Which of the following does the road sign given in the picture indicate?

A) Cattles may be crossing ahead

B) There are herders present on the road ahead

C) A farmhouse is located ahead

D) A cattle herd is located on the road ahead

40

When is the best time to return to the right lane after passing a car?

A) When you see the other car's headlights come on

B) Right after you have put your turn signal on

C) When you have turned your headlights on

D) When you can see the other car's front bumper in your mirror

CONTINUE ▶

SECTION 2

#	Answer	Topic	Subtopic	#	Answer	Topic	Subtopic	#	Answer	Topic	Subtopic	#	Answer	Topic	Subtopic
1	A	T03	S03674	11	D	T03	S03674	21	D	T03	S03676	31	B	T03	S03675
2	D	T03	S03674	12	C	T44	S44840	22	C	T03	S03676	32	D	T03	S03675
3	B	T44	S44837	13	B	T03	S03676	23	A	T03	S03676	33	C	T03	S03674
4	B	T03	S03675	14	B	T03	S03676	24	A	T03	S03673	34	D	T03	S03675
5	D	T44	S44839	15	D	T03	S03673	25	C	T03	S03674	35	D	T03	S03675
6	A	T03	S03676	16	A	T03	S03674	26	B	T03	S03676	36	B	T03	S03675
7	D	T03	S03676	17	C	T03	S03676	27	C	T44	S44839	37	A	T03	S03675
8	B	T03	S03675	18	C	T03	S03674	28	D	T03	S03674	38	A	T03	S03675
9	C	T03	S03675	19	A	T03	S03675	29	D	T03	S03673	39	A	T03	S03674
10	B	T03	S03676	20	D	T03	S03674	30	D	T03	S03674	40	D	T03	S03675

Topics & Subtopics

Code	Description	Code	Description
S03	USA DMV	S44	TX DMV
S03673	Alcohol and Drug	S44837	Alcohol and Drug
S03674	Road Signs	S44839	Rules and Laws
S03675	Rules and Laws	S44840	Safety
S03676	Safety		

CONTINUE ▶

TEST DIRECTION

DIRECTIONS

Read the questions carefully and then choose the ONE best answer to each question.

Be sure to allocate your time carefully so you are able to complete the entire test within the testing session. You may go back and review your answers at any time.

You may use any available space in your test booklet for scratch work.

Questions in this booklet are not actual test questions but they are the samples for commonly asked questions.

This test aims to cover all topics which may appear on the actual test. However some topics may not be covered.

Studying this booklet will be preparing you for the actual test. It will not guarantee improving your test score but it will help you pass your exam on the first attempt.

Some useful tips for answering multiple choice questions;

- Start with the questions that you can easily answer.

- Underline the keywords in the question.

- Be sure to read all the choices given.

- Watch for keywords such as NOT, always, only, all, never, completely.

- Do not forget to answer every question.

CONTINUE ▶

1

What does it mean when the road is marked with a solid yellow line and a broken yellow line on your side?

A) You may pass if the traffic is clear.

B) You may pass if you are on an expressway.

C) You may only pass in an emergency.

D) You may only pass at an intersection.

2

In which of the following instances a blind person would legally have the right-of-way when crossing the street?

A) When he is wearing dark-colored glasses

B) When he is wearing light-colored clothing

C) When he is using a white or metallic cane or a guide dog leading him

D) When he is helped by another person

3

A 16-year old minor can apply for a provisional driving license in Texas. He will be using the said type of license until 18 years of age.

Which of the following refers to the number of passengers that a driver with a provisional license can carry?

A) 1

B) 2

C) 3

D) 4

4

What is the best thing that you should do if you are being tailgated while you were driving?

A) You should speed up.

B) You should call the police.

C) You should maintain your speed, signal and change lanes if possible.

D) You should decrease your speed and flash your brake lights by pumping the brakes.

5

Which of the following statements is correct about blood alcohol content (BAC)?

A) A chemical test for BAC is needed as evidence for an alcohol conviction.

B) The physical fitness of a person reduces BAC levels.

C) Having a cold shower or coffee after drinking will lower your BAC.

D) The purpose of a "breathalyzer" is to test the blood alcohol content of a person.

CONTINUE ▶

6

Which of the following should a motorist do when approaching a bicyclist?

A) The motorist should swerve into the opposite lane.

B) The motorist should speed up to pass him.

C) The motorist should exercise extreme caution.

D) The motorist should proceed as usual.

7

Which of the following should you do to avoid glare from headlights of an oncoming vehicle?

A) You should keep glancing to the side of the road.

B) You should keep your focus on the center line on the road.

C) You should flash your high beams.

D) You should switch off your headlights.

8

What does the symbol given above indicate?

A) No driving zone

B) You can only go left or right

C) There is a narrow bridge ahead

D) There is a Y intersection ahead

9

Which of the following should be the best action as you are approaching an intersection, while the traffic light is changing from green to yellow?

A) You should drive faster to beat the red light.

B) You should be prepared to stop in the center of the intersection.

C) You should step on the brakes sharply to stop.

D) You should be prepared to stop before the intersection.

10

Which of the following does this traffic sign mean?

A) Two-way traffic ahead
B) Divided highway ends
C) Keep to the right
D) One-way traffic ahead

11

Which of the following best describes a work safety zone sign?

A) Orange and diamond shaped
B) Green and diamond shaped
C) Black and white and can be different shapes
D) Have a checker pattern on them

12

Space cushion is defined as the distance you maintain between you and the cars surrounding you in order to allow you to easily maneuver in any situation.

What is the advantage of having a space cushion around your vehicle?

A) Other drivers can insert in front of you, improving traffic flow.
B) You can have time to react if another driver makes a mistake.
C) In case of a collision, it inflates to protect you from injury.
D) You can drive faster.

13

If a pedestrian is walking on a road with no sidewalks, which side should he/she walk?

A) At the side of the road with the least traffic
B) At the side of the road facing the oncoming traffic
C) At the same side of the road where the traffic is moving
D) At the side of the road with the most traffic

14

A driver must present his license upon inspection by law enforcement. If it is found that the driver lacks a license, a fine will be given.

Which of the following refers to the amount that is fined for the driver who is found guilty of driving without a license?

A) $100.00
B) $200.00
C) $300.00
D) $500.00

15

In a parking space reserved for disabled people, which of the following is the right thing to do by a non-disabled driver?

A) He may park in an emergency.
B) He may not stop or park, but may stand in an emergency.
C) He may not park, but stop in an emergency.
D) He may neither park, stop nor stand.

16

In which of the following situations are you allowed to left turn on red unless prohibited by a sign?

A) Except in crosswalks
B) Except in school zones
C) Except when prohibited by a traffic sign, you may left turn on red from a one-way road to a one-way road
D) Except when prohibited by a traffic sign, you may left turn on red from a two-way road to one-way road.

17

Which of the following is the exact meaning of the road sign shown above?

A) Pedestrians ahead
B) Flagger ahead
C) School crossing ahead
D) End of construction zone

CONTINUE ▶

18

What does the traffic sign illustrated above means?

A) Do not drink if you are going to drive.

B) You are approaching a hill.

C) Road curves ahead.

D) Slippery when wet.

19

Consider a situation wherein you are driving in the middle lane on a three-lane expressway, and then a car begins to pass you on the right. As a driver, what should your action be?

A) It is okay as long as he does it on a limited access highway.

B) It is wrong because "pass to the left" is a firm rule.

C) It is wrong because he is passing you in your "blind spot."

D) It is okay if no signs forbid passing on the right.

20

Which of the following is the meaning of the road sign shown above?

A) There is a four-way intersection ahead.

B) Another road joins from the right.

C) The lane you are traveling on ends ahead.

D) You must drive either left or right ahead.

21

How long will it take for the alcohol to leave your bloodstream if you had three beers in the past hour?

A) Three

B) Five

C) Eight

D) Twelve

22

What does the road sign shown above tells you?

A) You are approaching a blasting zone.

B) You are already near an intersection.

C) You are approaching a railroad crossing.

D) You are already near a crosswalk.

23

A white line can be seen on roads used to separate traffic lanes. What is the purpose of this?

A) It indicates separate lanes of traffic moving in different directions.

B) It indicates separate lanes of traffic moving in the same direction.

C) It indicates that you must drive on the left side of the line.

D) None of the above.

24

In which of the following situations are you allowed to pass vehicles?

A) You may pass vehicles going in the same direction as you are going to the right.

B) You may pass vehicles only if the other driver signals it is safe.

C) You may pass vehicles going in the same direction as you are going to the left.

D) You may pass vehicles whenever you have the opportunity to do so.

25

Rumble strips which are also known as sleeper lines or wake up calls alert inattentive drivers for potential dangers.

What is the purpose of rumble strips?

A) To test the vehicle's shock absorbers.

B) To look for traffic by using your inside rear-view mirror.

C) To notify sleepy or distracted drivers through sound and vibration that they are approaching a stop sign or signal or their vehicle has left the travel lane

D) To alert the driver that he is speeding

26

Blood alcohol content (BAC) is independent of the _____.

What is missing from the statement above?

A) amount of time passing between drinks

B) physical fitness of an individual

C) amount of alcohol consumed

D) body weight of an individual

27

Vehicle parking laws are well-stated, especially in densely populated areas. Proper parking of vehicles will help ease traffic and restore order in the roads, possibly avoiding other accidents.

Where is a driver not allowed to park in Texas?

A) Within an intersection

B) In the middle of the street

C) On the pedestrian lane

D) All of the above

28

Which of the following should not be done by a driver when changing lanes?

A) Checking over his/her right or left shoulder when checking for blind spots

B) Checking for other drivers shifting into the same lane

C) Changing lanes in a junction

D) Giving signals when changing lanes

CONTINUE ▶

29

What is the meaning of the road sign shown above?

A) Pedestrian crossing

B) No turns are allowed on this road.

C) Winding road ahead

D) Check brakes

31

In which of the following instances should you use your horn?

A) When another vehicle is in your way

B) In preventing a collision

C) When another driver makes a mistake

D) When a pedestrian is crossing the street

30

What does the road sign shown above mean?

A) Stop only for traffic at an intersection.

B) Come to a full stop, then go when it is safe to do so.

C) Proceed carefully through the intersection.

D) Slow down and prepare to stop if there is any vehicle approaching you.

32

What does the sign shown above mean?

A) Merge

B) Reduction in lanes

C) Stop sign ahead

D) Rail road ahead

CONTINUE ▶

33

Which of the following is the best thing to do if you come to an intersection which is blocked by other traffic?

A) Go slowly until the traffic ahead moves.
B) Stay out of the intersection and wait until you can pass through.
C) Get closer to the other car.
D) Make the cars move up by blowing your horn.

34

A driver must pay attention while on the road for safety. It is necessary to apply your safety driving skills when needed, avoiding conflict and accident.

Which of the following actions should be taken when a driver from the other lane is coming over towards your lane?

A) Pull to the right and slow down
B) Pull to the left and come to a stop
C) Stop on your lane and wait for the other vehicle
D) Continue on your way and take note of the plate number for future reference

35

Road signs are important to remind the drivers of the road conditions ahead of time. It will help the driver prepare for the surroundings on the road or other concerns that must be paid attention.

Which of the following refers to the road sign provided in the picture above?

A) Narrow bridge ahead
B) Bridge construction ahead
C) Road is narrowing ahead
D) Road will narrow for 5 miles ahead

CONTINUE ▶

36

Which of the following is possible when driving on gravel or dirt roads?

A) The visibility is better.

B) The road is safer to drive than on pavement.

C) Your tires can grip the road better than on pavement.

D) Tires have lesser traction when on gravel than on normal roads, so you must drive slower.

37

A **hit-and-run accident** is a case that usually refers to the car accidents wherein a car driver runs off from the victim that he might have accidentally hit while driving.

Which of the following is the amount stated to be fined in Texas for a hit-and-run case where the complainant is injured?

A) $1,000.00

B) $3,000.00

C) $5,000.00

D) $10,000.00

38

In some cases, drivers must take note of which signs will take precedence over the other. In case of a stop sign and a traffic light, it is indicative of following the traffic light to take over the stop sign since the stop sign is contained as an action from the traffic light.

Which of the following will take precedence over the others?

A) Traffic signal

B) Road sign

C) Police officer

D) Traffic enforcer

39

When is passing always forbidden?

A) When you are on a one-way street which has two lanes

B) When a vehicle ahead is stopped for a pedestrian in a crosswalk

C) When a vehicle ahead is going to park parallel to the curb

D) When a vehicle ahead is making a left turn

Which of the following about the blind spots
is correct?

A) Blind spots are terminated if you have
   one outside mirror on each side of the
   car.

B) Large trucks have greater blind spots as
   compared to passenger vehicles.

C) A driver can check blind spots by
   looking in the rearview mirrors.

D) A driver can check blind spots by
   sounding the horn.

SECTION 3

#	Answer	Topic	Subtopic	#	Answer	Topic	Subtopic	#	Answer	Topic	Subtopic	#	Answer	Topic	Subtopic
1	A	T03	S03676	11	A	T03	S03676	21	A	T03	S03673	31	B	T03	S03676
2	C	T03	S03676	12	B	T03	S03676	22	C	T03	S03674	32	B	T03	S03674
3	A	T44	S44839	13	B	T03	S03675	23	B	T03	S03675	33	B	T03	S03675
4	C	T03	S03676	14	B	T44	S44839	24	C	T03	S03675	34	A	T03	S03676
5	D	T03	S03673	15	D	T03	S03675	25	C	T03	S03676	35	A	T03	S03674
6	C	T03	S03676	16	C	T03	S03674	26	B	T03	S03673	36	D	T03	S03676
7	A	T03	S03676	17	B	T03	S03674	27	A	T44	S44839	37	C	T44	S44839
8	B	T03	S03674	18	D	T03	S03676	28	C	T03	S03676	38	C	T03	S03675
9	D	T03	S03675	19	D	T03	S03675	29	C	T03	S03674	39	B	T03	S03675
10	C	T03	S03674	20	D	T03	S03674	30	B	T03	S03674	40	B	T03	S03676

Topics & Subtopics

Code	Description	Code	Description
S03	USA DMV	S03676	Safety
S03673	Alcohol and Drug	S44	TX DMV
S03674	Road Signs	S44839	Rules and Laws
S03675	Rules and Laws		

CONTINUE ▶

TEST DIRECTION

DIRECTIONS

Read the questions carefully and then choose the ONE best answer to each question.

Be sure to allocate your time carefully so you are able to complete the entire test within the testing session. You may go back and review your answers at any time.

You may use any available space in your test booklet for scratch work.

Questions in this booklet are not actual test questions but they are the samples for commonly asked questions.

This test aims to cover all topics which may appear on the actual test. However some topics may not be covered.

Studying this booklet will be preparing you for the actual test. It will not guarantee improving your test score but it will help you pass your exam on the first attempt.

Some useful tips for answering multiple choice questions;

- Start with the questions that you can easily answer.

- Underline the keywords in the question.

- Be sure to read all the choices given.

- Watch for keywords such as NOT, always, only, all, never, completely.

- Do not forget to answer every question.

CONTINUE ▶

1

What should you do if you want to overtake and pass another vehicle?

A) You should shift lanes quickly so that the other driver will see you.

B) You should give a signal and pass when it is safe to do so.

C) You should wait for the other driver to give a signal.

D) You should stay close behind so you will only need lesser time to pass.

2

Which of the following limits your concentration, perception, judgment, and memory?

A) A blood alcohol level higher than the legal limit

B) Even the smallest amount of alcohol

C) A blood alcohol level higher than 0.05

D) A blood alcohol level equivalent to five bottles of liquor

3

When are you allowed to proceed if the traffic prevents you from crossing all the way across a set of railroad tracks?

A) If there are no trains in sight

B) If at least half of your vehicle can cross the tracks

C) If there is room for your vehicle to be on the other side

D) If an incoming train is not moving fast enough to be a danger

4

Consider a situation wherein you are approaching an intersection on a two-way road and making a left turn. In this case, who has the right-of-way?

A) The traffic traveling in the opposite direction and going straight

B) The traffic traveling in the opposite direction and turning right

C) Both a and b

D) None of the above

5

When must you yield the right-of-way to an approaching vehicle?

A) When you are turning left

B) When you are going straight ahead

C) When you are already in a traffic circle

D) When you are already in an intersection

6

High beam is described as the brightest setting of the headlights of a vehicle.

When is high beam should not be used?

A) When it rains

B) When it snows

C) When it is foggy

D) All of the above

7

Which of the following should you do if you are in the center lane of an expressway and vehicles are continually passing you on the right and the left?

A) Move to the lane on your right

B) Move to the lane on your left

C) Stay in the center lane

D) Increase your speed

8

Driving while drowsy is just like drinking alcohol and other drugs. What is the effect of it on driving?

A) Make you more focused

B) Help you to be a better driver

C) Make you feel better

D) Impair your judgment

CONTINUE ▶

9

Even if there is a "no stopping" sign, there are instances that a policeman would allow you to stop at this point. Why is this so?

A) You may stop only to discharge passengers.

B) You may stop only to avoid conflict with other traffic.

C) You may stop only for less than 5 minutes.

D) You may stop long enough to unload packages.

10

What is the penalty for driving under the influence of alcohol or other drugs?

A) A mandatory fine

B) Driver license revocation

C) Possible imprisonment

D) All of the above

11

What is the meaning of a flashing yellow light?

A) Merging traffic

B) Come to a full stop

C) Pedestrian crossing

D) Proceed with caution

12

What should you do if a fire truck is responding to an emergency?

A) You should stay back 3 to 6 seconds.

B) You should stay back at least 200 feet.

C) You should stay back at least 500 feet.

D) You should stay back at least 1000 feet.

13

Hydroplaning occurs when a water layer builds up in between the road surface and the wheels of the vehicle.

In which of the following instances is hydroplaning possible?

A) Tires lose contact with the road surface

B) Spray from large trucks reducing visibility

C) Rain cannot be cleared off on a windshield by the windshield wipers

D) Tires having strong traction with the road surface

14

The Texas Department of Public Safety, or TxDPS, is the regulating government body for vehicle regulation and law enforcement. Due to its nature, the TxDPS adds points to a driver's record according to the number of violations and accidents made in three years.

Which of the following refers to the number of accumulated points stated by TxDPS for a driver to be assessed with a surcharge?

A) 6

B) 4

C) 2

D) 8

15

Which among the following determines the effects of alcohol on its user?

A) The amount of food in the stomach

B) The body weight of an individual

C) The amount of time between drinks

D) All of the above

16

You are in an intersection where there is no stop line, but there are stop sign and a crosswalk.

Which of the following should you do?

A) You must stop with your front wheels in the crosswalk.

B) You must stop 50 feet prior to the intersection.

C) You must stop before the crosswalk.

D) You must halt driving where you think the stop line would be.

17

Which of the following should you do while driving in inclement weather?

A) Steer off the road

B) Drive in low gear

C) Steer and brake smoothly

D) Drive in high gear

18

What will most likely happen if you drive slower than the flow of the traffic?

A) You will be showing defensive driving techniques.

B) You will improve traffic flow.

C) You will interfere with traffic and receive a ticket.

D) Other vehicles will not overtake.

19

Which statement about drinking alcohol and driving is true?

A) If you can walk a straight line after drinking, it is safe to drive.

B) Alcohol affects judgment, which is needed for driving safely.

C) If you are under the legal blood alcohol concentration limit, your driving isn't impaired.

D) If you are of legal age, driving while drunk is safe.

20

Vehicle headlights help the drivers see the road more properly. Although there are street lights in most areas, it is recommended and required to turn it on half an hour after sunset.

Which of the following is the set time where you can turn off your headlights in Texas?

A) Half hour before sunrise

B) One hour before sunrise

C) Two hours before sunrise

D) Keep it lit

21

Which of the following is correct in making a right turn?

A) Your car must be close to the center of the street.

B) Your car must be passing the center of the intersection when you start turning.

C) Your car must be near the left side of the street.

D) Your car must be close to the right side of the street.

22

Which of the following statements is true about using bicycles during the night?

A) Motorists should know that all bicycles used at night must have a front headlight and a red tail light.

B) Motorists should know that all bicycles used at night must have a reflective handlebar grips.

C) Motorists should know that all bicycles used at night must have brake lights.

D) Motorists should know that all bicycles used at night must have white reflectors on the front and rear fenders.

23

A red light indicates a stop sign when you are on the road. Your vehicle must stop and wait until the light turns green again before moving forward.

Which of the following situations will nullify the red light sign when you are turning?

A) From one-way street to two-way street

B) From one-way street to one-way street

C) From two-way street to one-way street

D) From two-way street to two-way street

24

A driver who intends to turn has to signal the vehicles beforehand. It will act as a warning for the vehicles to slow down while you take the time to turn.

Which of the following is the appropriate distance where you first turn on your signal light continuously at slow speed?

A) 50 feet

B) 100 feet

C) 200 feet

D) 500 feet

CONTINUE ▶

25

What does the traffic sign shown above mean?

A) There is one-way traffic ahead.

B) Divided highway ends ahead.

C) There is a divided highway ahead.

D) Four-lane highway ahead.

26

In which of the following instances do collisions happen more often?

A) When one lane of traffic has a greater speed than the other lanes

B) When all cars are traveling about the same speed

C) When one car is traveling slower or faster than the traffic flow

D) When cars on the road are giving signals when changing lanes

27

Which of the following road signals is used on some highways to direct drivers into the proper lanes for turning?

A) Flashing red lights

B) White lines on the side of the road

C) White arrows in the middle of the lanes

D) Flashing yellow lights

28

What should a driver do when approaching a junction where the traffic light has changed to yellow?

A) The driver must clear the junction before the light turns red.

B) The driver should proceed with caution.

C) The driver should be prepared for a safe stop and wait until the light turns green.

D) The driver may quickly proceed through the junction without any caution.

29

What is the meaning of the road sign shown above?

A) No Right Turn

B) Stop Sign Ahead

C) Divided Highway

D) No Left Turn

30

What should you do if you notice that the rear wheels of your car are skidding to the right while you are driving?

A) The gas pedal should be released and turn the steering wheel to the left.

B) The gas pedal should be released and turn the steering wheel to the right.

C) You should stop immediately.

D) You should slow down.

31

Which of the following is a result of drinking alcohol and taking a precription drug or over the counter medicine?

A) Taking alcohol and medicine simultaneously could multiply the effects of the alcohol.

B) Taking a prescribed medicine can reduce the effect of the alcohol.

C) The alcohol helps the medicine cure the cold.

D) There is no effect because they are different substances.

32

When can a driver park in a space reserved for people with disabilities?

A) If someone in the driver's immediate family is disabled

B) Regardless who is in the vehicle

C) If the vehicle displays license plates for the disabled and is carrying the disabled person named on the registration

D) Only if the driver is disabled

CONTINUE ▶

33

How can you prevent your drowsiness when driving on long trips?

A) By constantly moving your eyes from side to side as you drive.

B) By stopping and taking a rest at regular intervals.

C) By switching on your car radio.

D) By decreasing your speed so you can react better.

34

As you were driving, you observed that the traffic light has a green arrow and a red light. What does this mean?

A) Vehicles moving in any direction must stop.

B) You may only drive straight ahead.

C) You are only allowed to drive in the direction of the green arrow.

D) You must wait for a green light.

35

Which of the following is the correct order of the traffic lights from top to bottom?

A) Green, red, yellow

B) Red, yellow, green

C) Red, green, yellow

D) Yellow, green, red

36

If you want to turn right at the next intersection, what should you do?

A) You should switch on your turn signal at least 50 feet before the turn.

B) You should switch on your turn signal as soon as you see cars behind you.

C) You should switch on your turn signal when you reach the intersection.

D) You should switch on your turn signal at least 100 feet before the turn.

SECTION 4

#	Answer	Topic	Subtopic	#	Answer	Topic	Subtopic	#	Answer	Topic	Subtopic	#	Answer	Topic	Subtopic
1	B	T03	S03676	10	D	T03	S03673	19	B	T03	S03673	28	C	T03	S03675
2	B	T03	S03673	11	D	T03	S03674	20	A	T44	S44839	29	A	T03	S03674
3	C	T03	S03674	12	C	T03	S03675	21	D	T03	S03676	30	B	T03	S03676
4	C	T03	S03675	13	B	T03	S03676	22	A	T03	S03676	31	A	T03	S03673
5	A	T03	S03675	14	A	T44	S44839	23	B	T44	S44839	32	C	T03	S03675
6	D	T03	S03675	15	D	T03	S03673	24	B	T44	S44838	33	B	T03	S03676
7	A	T03	S03674	16	C	T03	S03676	25	B	T03	S03674	34	C	T03	S03674
8	D	T03	S03673	17	C	T03	S03676	26	C	T03	S03676	35	B	T03	S03674
9	B	T03	S03674	18	C	T03	S03676	27	C	T03	S03674	36	D	T03	S03675

Topics & Subtopics

Code	Description	Code	Description
S03	USA DMV	S03676	Safety
S03673	Alcohol and Drug	S44	TX DMV
S03674	Road Signs	S44838	Road Signs
S03675	Rules and Laws	S44839	Rules and Laws

CONTINUE ▶

TEST DIRECTION

DIRECTIONS

Read the questions carefully and then choose the ONE best answer to each question.

Be sure to allocate your time carefully so you are able to complete the entire test within the testing session. You may go back and review your answers at any time.

You may use any available space in your test booklet for scratch work.

Questions in this booklet are not actual test questions but they are the samples for commonly asked questions.

This test aims to cover all topics which may appear on the actual test. However some topics may not be covered.

Studying this booklet will be preparing you for the actual test. It will not guarantee improving your test score but it will help you pass your exam on the first attempt.

Some useful tips for answering multiple choice questions;

- Start with the questions that you can easily answer.

- Underline the keywords in the question.

- Be sure to read all the choices given.

- Watch for keywords such as NOT, always, only, all, never, completely.

- Do not forget to answer every question.

1

Which vehicles must stop at all railroad crossing?

A) Motorcycles

B) Pickup trucks

C) School buses and passenger buses

D) Vehicles towing a trailer

2

Which of the following is the meaning of a "no parking" sign at a certain location?

A) You may never stop your vehicle there.

B) You are allowed to park there if the driver remains in the vehicle.

C) You are allowed to leave your vehicle unattended for less than 5 minutes.

D) You are allowed to stop temporarily to drop people off or pick them up, but you still can't load or unload things from cars or trucks.

3

Seat belt is a safety device on vehicles used to fasten the passenger of a vehicle against risky movement that may result during an accident, collision or an abrupt stop.

When can seat belts be most effective as injury preventive devices?

A) When they are worn by the driver and passengers whenever they are in the car.

B) When they are worn by passengers when they are on a long drive.

C) When they are worn by the person driving the car.

D) When they are worn by all the occupants of a car being driven on an expressway.

4

What is the purpose of the road sign illustrated above?

A) To prevent entrance to the road construction areas

B) To prevent entrance to full parking lots

C) To prevent entrance to dead-end streets

D) To prevent wrong-way entrance on expressway ramps and on one-way streets

What should you do if there is an oncoming car from behind at night?

A) If you are within 100 feet away from the other car, you should lower your high beam headlights.
B) If you are within 500 feet away from the other car, you should lower your high beam headlights.
C) If you are within 200 feet away from the other car, you should lower your high beam headlights.
D) If you are within 50 feet away from the other car, you should lower your high beam headlights.

The area where the person's perspective is blocked is called the **blind spot**.

Which of the following should you check for you to see vehicles in your blind spot?

A) You should check the outside rearview mirror.
B) You should check the inside rearview mirror.
C) You should check over your shoulders.
D) You should fully look at the back seat part of your car.

CONTINUE ▶

7

Which of the following is the best action of a driver when approaching a traffic control signal that is not in operation?

A) The driver should not stop if the intersection is clear.

B) The driver should come to a full stop and yield the right-of-way before entering the intersection.

C) The driver should drive quickly through the intersection to get out of the way of other vehicles.

D) The driver should continue driving to avoid other vehicles getting in the way.

8

What is the term used for the amount of alcohol in the blood?

A) Implied consent (IC)

B) Blood alcohol concentration (BAC)

C) Rate of alcohol consumption (RAC)

D) Alcohol consumption rate (ACR)

9

Which of the following is correct if two cars arrive at a four-way stop at the same time?

A) The car on the right should yield to the car on the left.

B) The driver should move fast before the other driver makes his decision.

C) The driver should make hand motions to convey his intentions to the other driver.

D) The car on the left must yield to the car on the right.

10

A driver who is convicted for a Driving While Intoxicated (DWI) in Texas is jailed, fined, and suspended for a varying amount of money and time depending on the number of offense made.

Which of the following is the number of days that a second-time offender for a DWI will get at maximum?

A) 180 days

B) 120 days

C) 90 days

D) 60 days

CONTINUE ▶

11

What is the most important thing to consider about speed management and curves?

A) Accelerate gently before you enter the curve.

B) As you enter the curve, observe the posted speed limit of the roadway, and then decrease the speed at the sharpest part of the curve.

C) Consider the posted speed limit of the roadway while driving before, throughout, and after the curve.

D) Drivers should slow down before entering a curve.

12

How many hours can a human body dispose of alcohol in 12 ounces of beer?

A) Five hours

B) One hour

C) One day

D) Five minutes

13

Which of the following statements is correct about excessive speed?

A) It saves time so you can arrive to your destination earlier.

B) It increases the possibility of serious bodily injuries and death.

C) It helps you to maneuver around obstacles.

D) Speeding is generally considered excessive if you drive 50+ mph over the limit.

14

Which of the following is the most appropriate thing to do while you are entering an interstate highway?

A) You should decrease your speed and merge when the way is clear.

B) You should check for cars and reduce speed to 25 mph before entering the traffic lane.

C) You should stop for a while, check for cars and enter when safe.

D) You should check for cars, match the flow of traffic by increasing your speed and merge when the way is clear.

CONTINUE ▶

15

What should you do when you are changing lanes?

A) You should slow down.

B) You should look over your shoulder to make sure that the lane is clear.

C) You should check the inside rearview mirror.

D) You should change lanes immediately right after passing a vehicle.

16

When it rains, the road becomes slippery. Which of the following should you do if the road is slippery?

A) You should avoid making fast brakes and fast turns.

B) While going uphill, you should test your tires' traction.

C) Decrease the distance when looking ahead of your vehicle.

D) Increase the distance when looking ahead of your vehicle.

17

Which of the following statements is correct when blocking a junction during "rush hour" traffic?

A) It is not allowed under any circumstances, even if your light is green.

B) It is not allowed unless you have the right of way or a green light.

C) It is not allowed unless you entered the junction on a green light.

D) It is allowed under any circumstance, even if your light is red.

18

Which of the following signs are usually diamond shaped with black lettering or symbols on a yellow background?

A) Service signs

B) Destination signs

C) Regulatory signs

D) Warning signs

19

What is the most appropriate thing to do if you are driving and there is an incoming ambulance from the opposite direction?

A) You should slow down and pull over to the right.

B) You should stop immediately.

C) Just keep driving.

D) You should speed up and drive faster.

20

In your direction, there are two traffic lanes. As you are driving along the left lane, many vehicles are passing you on the right. Behind you, there is a driver who is trying to drive faster.

Which of the following should you do in this situation?

A) Move onto the left shoulder to let the other cars overtake.

B) Drive into the right lane when you think it is already safe.

C) Keep driving in your lane so you do not block the traffic flow.

D) Immediately drive into the right lane.

CONTINUE ▶

21

Road signs are indications of areas, rules, or laws that a driver must remember when passing by the road. It reminds the driver for safety and considerations.

Which of the following is the indication of the road sign in the picture?

A) An underpass ahead; vertical clearance of 11 feet and 6 inches

B) A mall parking ahead; vertical clearance of 11 feet and 6 inches

C) A bridge ahead; road width of 11 feet and 6 inches

D) A tunnel ahead; road width of 11 feet and 6 inches

22

Which of the following is the most appropriate thing to do if you are driving on the freeway behind a large truck?

A) You should drive to the right side of the truck and wait to pass.

B) You should drive closer behind the truck than for a passenger vehicle.

C) You should drive farther behind the truck as compared to a passenger vehicle.

D) You should drive to the left side of the truck and wait to pass.

23

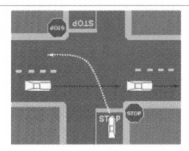

The driver of a vehicle must come to a complete stop whenever a complete stop sign is present on the road or an intersection. This is to give caution to the drivers if there are no stoplights present or if there is an inspection to be held.

Which of the following is the car that has to pass first?

A) The car on the left, then the car on the right

B) The car on the right , then the car on the left

C) Whichever wants to go first

D) They can pass at the same time if it is convenient

24

Which of the following statements is correct about large trucks?

A) Large trucks take longer to stop than passenger vehicles.

B) Large trucks are easier to maneuver than passenger vehicles.

C) All large trucks have air brakes which allow them to stop quickly.

D) Large trucks take a shorter time to stop as compared to other vehicles.

Which of the following is the meaning of the road sign shown above?

A) Pedestrian crossing ahead.

B) Pedestrians must not cross here.

C) Pedestrians are walking along the road ahead.

D) Pedestrians are running along the road ahead.

DRUG-IMPAIRED DRIVING

Which of the following about driving and taking medications is correct?

A) It is safe to drive when taking any medications.

B) Usually, medicines for cold can make a person feel sleepy.

C) If recommended by a doctor, medicines are safe to take at any time.

D) If taken in the exact dosages, over the counter medications cannot negatively affect driving ability.

27

Which of the following is correct when a driver changes lanes?

A) Rear-view mirrors never have a blind spot.

B) Automobiles with two mirrors on the outside still have blind spots.

C) The driver only needs to turn and look over his/her right shoulder for lane changes to the left or right.

D) The driver should look over his/her left shoulder for right lane change and his/her right shoulder for a left lane change.

28

Which of the following is the correct definition of a crosswalk?

A) It is an area designated for road construction workers.

B) It is the area where pedestrians are allowed to cross the roadway.

C) It is the other name for a four-way intersection.

D) It is an area where drivers are allowed to park.

29

The qualitative and quantitave ways used to characterize, measure and identify certain chemical compounds on a test sample is called a **chemical test**.

What is the purpose of a chemical test when a driver drank a liquor?

A) It is used to measure vision.

B) It is used to measure reaction time.

C) It is used to measure blood alcohol content.

D) It is used to measure driving ability.

30

In which of the following areas you may never park?

A) At the entrance of a building

B) On a one-way street

C) In a crosswalk

D) Within 50 feet of a fire hydrant

31

What should you do if you are approaching someone using a white cane or guide dog?

A) You should stop driving until the person is well away from the roadway or path of travel.

B) You should carefully drive around them.

C) You should honk your horn as you are passing them.

D) You should avoid them and continue driving.

32

Which of the following is the meaning of the road sign shown above?

A) School crossing ahead

B) Hiking trails ahead

C) Pedestrians crossing ahead

D) Intersection ahead

33

Where do you think you are driving if you are in the far right lane of a four lane freeway and notice thick broken white lines on the left side of your lane?

A) You are driving in a special lane for slow moving vehicles.

B) You are traveling in the carpool lane and must merge into the next lane.

C) You are driving in an exit lane.

D) You are driving in an intersection.

34

Which of the following is true about the effect of alcohol on driving skills and judgment?

A) It harms both driving skills and judgment.

B) It enhances driving skills, but harms your judgment.

C) It does not affect judgment, but it harms driving skills.

D) It has no effect on either driving skills or judgement.

35

Which of the following should a driver do if an approaching train is near enough or going fast enough to be a danger?

A) The driver must cross the tracks at your own risk.

B) The driver must slow down and proceed with caution.

C) The driver must find an alternative route across tracks.

D) The driver must not cross the tracks until the train has completely passed

36

Which of the following is the meaning of the road sign illustrated above?

A) Hill ahead.

B) Truckstop ahead.

C) Trucks are NOT allowed.

D) Trucks under 18,000 pounds are allowed.

SECTION 5

#	Answer	Topic	Subtopic	#	Answer	Topic	Subtopic	#	Answer	Topic	Subtopic	#	Answer	Topic	Subtopic
1	C	T03	S03675	10	A	T44	S44837	19	A	T03	S03676	28	B	T03	S03674
2	D	T03	S03674	11	D	T03	S03676	20	B	T03	S03676	29	C	T03	S03673
3	A	T03	S03676	12	B	T03	S03673	21	A	T03	S03674	30	C	T03	S03675
4	D	T03	S03674	13	B	T03	S03676	22	C	T03	S03676	31	A	T03	S03675
5	C	T03	S03675	14	D	T03	S03675	23	A	T03	S03675	32	A	T03	S03674
6	C	T03	S03676	15	B	T03	S03675	24	A	T03	S03676	33	C	T03	S03676
7	B	T03	S03675	16	A	T03	S03676	25	A	T03	S03674	34	A	T03	S03673
8	B	T03	S03673	17	A	T03	S03675	26	B	T03	S03673	35	D	T03	S03676
9	D	T03	S03675	18	D	T03	S03674	27	B	T03	S03675	36	A	T03	S03674

Topics & Subtopics

Code	Description	Code	Description
S03	USA DMV	S03676	Safety
S03673	Alcohol and Drug	S44	TX DMV
S03674	Road Signs	S44837	Alcohol and Drug
S03675	Rules and Laws		

CONTINUE ▶

Made in the USA
Coppell, TX
18 November 2022